plant parts

Stems and Trunks

Melanie Waldron

Raintree is an imprint of Capstone Global Library Limited, a company incorporated in England and Wales having its registered office at 7 Pilgrim Street, London, EC4V 6LB – Registered company number: 6695582

www.raintreepublishers.co.uk
myorders@raintreepublishers.co.uk

Text © Capstone Global Library Limited 2014
First published in hardback in 2014
The moral rights of the proprietor have been asserted.

Edited by Sian Smith and Adrian Vigliano
Designed by Cynthia Akiyoshi
Original illustrations © HL Studios
Illustrated by HL Studios
Picture research by Mica Brancic
Originated by Capstone Global Library Ltd
Printed in China by CTPS

ISBN 978 1 406 27481 3
17 16 15 14 13
10 9 8 7 6 5 4 3 2 1

British Library Cataloguing in Publication Data
Waldron, Melanie
Stems and trunks (Plant parts)
A full catalogue record for this book is available from the British Library.

Acknowledgements
We would like to thank the following for permission to reproduce photographs: Alamy p. 24 (© Grant Heilman Photography/Runk/Schoenberger); Capstone Publishers pp. 14, 15 (© Karon Dubke); Getty Images pp. 10 bottom, 11 bottom (Oxford Scientific/Martin Leigh); Naturepl.com pp. 6 (© Adrian Davies), 9 (© Phil Savoie or © Fekete Tibor), 18 (© Pete Cairns), 20 (Widstrand/© Wild Wonders of Europe), 21 (© Juan Carlos Munoz), 23 (© Visuals Unlimited), 27 (© Nick Garbutt), 28 (2020VISION/© Mark Hamblin), 19 top (© Juan Carlos Munoz), 5 top (© Eric Baccega); Shutterstock pp. 4 (© Matthew Connolly), 7 (© Zeljko Radojko), 12 (© Dr. Morley Read), 13 (© Andrew Ferguson), 17 (© Loskutnikov), 22 (© Alexey Kormakov), 26 (© Max Topchii), 10 top (© kentoh), 11 top (© photosync), 13 bottom (© MindStorm), 19 bottom (© Dec Hogan), 25 top (© wasanajai), 29 bottom (© fritz16), 29 top (© Sapsiwai), 5 bottom (© artjazz), Imprint page (© gillmar), title page (© SergeyIT).

Cover photograph reproduced with permission of Shutterstock (© SergeyIT).

We would like to thank Michael Bright for his invaluable help in the preparation of this book.

Every effort has been made to contact copyright holders of material reproduced in this book. Any omissions will be rectified in subsequent printings if notice is given to the publisher.

Contents

Some words are shown in bold, **like this**. You can find out what they mean by looking in the glossary.

Tiny stems, huge trunks

All sorts of plants, all over the world, have stems or trunks. They support the plant and help it to grow tall. They are filled with tiny tubes. Water and food can flow in these tubes to all the parts of the plant.

Giant sequoia trees have huge straight trunks.

Some plants, such as mosses, are tiny. They have very short, thin, bendy stems. Stems like these are sometimes called **stalks**. Other plants, such as giant sequoia trees, have huge stems called trunks that reach high into the air. Stalks, stems, and trunks all do the same job for the plant.

Horizontal stems

The Arctic willow is a tree that grows in the cold Arctic. Its trunk grows along the ground rather than up into the air. This keeps the plant out of cold, drying winds and helps it to survive.

Different plants

Flowers in a vase might have strong and straight stems. **Conifer** trees have single, straight trunks. **Broadleaved** tree trunks are often split into many branches. Bushes and shrubs have lots of thin, hard stems. It is difficult to tell where lawn grass stems are!

5

Important part to play

Stems and trunks are very important parts of plants. Plants also have other important parts to help them grow and survive. **Roots** hold the plant in the ground. They also take in water and **nutrients** from the soil for the plant to use.

Leaves make food for the plant. Flowers make seeds that can grow into new plants.

This oak tree has been uprooted. You can see some of its roots at the bottom of the trunk.

You can see how the leaves and the flowers grow from the stems of these sunflowers.

Different stems

Stems can look very different and be very different sizes. However, they all do the same jobs for each plant. A stem holds the plant up to help it get light. Stems also transport water and nutrients from the roots of the plant to all the places these are needed. Food made in the plant's leaves travels through the stem to every part of the plant.

Hidden underground

Water lilies have thick stems that stay buried in the mud at the bottom of ponds, lakes, and rivers. They have long stalks that float to the surface. The leaves and flowers grow from these long stalks.

1

Inside stems and trunks

There are lots of tiny tubes running up and down inside stems and trunks. **Xylem** tubes carry water from the roots. They deliver it around the plant. The leaves need water to mix with the food made there. This makes a sugary liquid called **sap**. **Phloem** tubes carry the sap around the plant.

This diagram shows the parts of a plant, and the tubes inside the stem. Older stems, such as tree trunks, have rings of xylem and phloem.

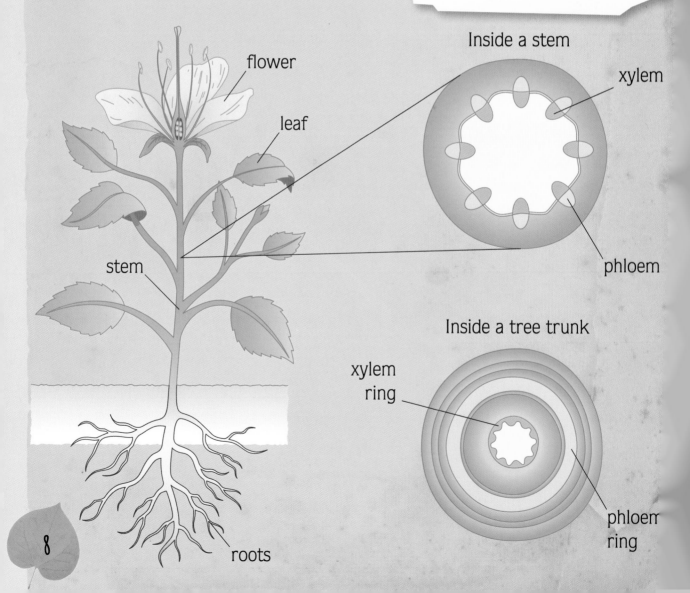

flower

leaf

Inside a stem

xylem

phloem

stem

roots

Inside a tree trunk

xylem
ring

phloem
ring

The heartwood of this oak tree is the dark wood in the centre. The sapwood is the lighter wood towards the outside.

Tree rings

Some parts of the world have warm summers and cold winters. In the spring, the tree grows quickly. This makes light-coloured rings of xylem and phloem. In summer, the growth slows down and the rings are darker.

Using sap

The sap from a sugar maple tree can be made into delicious maple syrup. To get the sap, people have to cut into the tree trunks until they reach the sapwood. The sap oozes out, and is boiled to become syrup.

As a tree ages, the rings in the centre of the trunk become solid. The tubes here stop carrying food and water. This part of the trunk is called **heartwood**.

Try this!

You can see where water moves up through a stem in this experiment.

You will need:

- a stick of celery
- a knife
- water
- a vase
- food colouring.

1 Take a stick of celery with leaves on. Ask an adult to help you cut a slice off the bottom of the celery. This will help the celery to take up water.

2 Mix some food colouring into a vase of water. Make sure that the water is a strong colour. Place the celery into the vase.

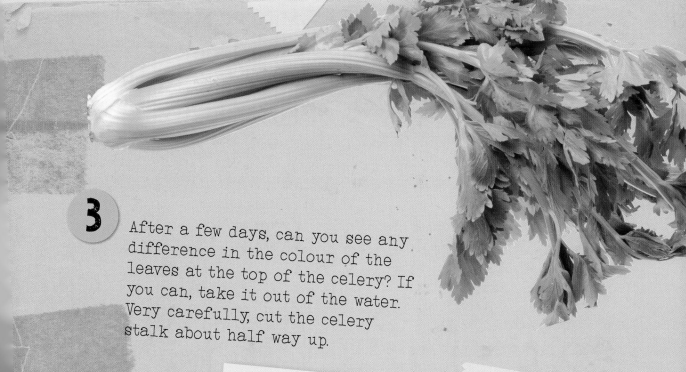

3 After a few days, can you see any difference in the colour of the leaves at the top of the celery? If you can, take it out of the water. Very carefully, cut the celery stalk about half way up.

4 Now look at the end of the stalk. Can you see little coloured holes? These are the xylem tubes. They are filled with the coloured water.

What next?

You could try this experiment again with some white flowers. What do you think might happen to the white petals?

Standing tall

Stems and trunks grow upwards to provide height for plants. The leaves can then take in as much light as possible. They need light, and a gas from the air called **carbon dioxide**, to make food for the plant.

Woody plants such as trees and shrubs have strong trunks and hardened stems. This means they can grow tall and support a lot of branches, leaves, and flowers.

Rainforests are full of tall trees. Some have trunks that push even higher, to help the tree catch more light and make more food.

Water support

Soft stems and stalks can stay upright because of the water inside them. The water makes their **cells** tight and strong. In times of **drought**, when there is little rainfall, the cells lose water. They become floppy and soft like a deflated balloon, so the plant droops over.

grape vine

Hang on!

Some plants grow high quickly, before their stems are ready to support them. They do this by growing long, thin **tendrils** from their stems. These tendrils curl around anything they find, and the plant is supported.

Try this!

Try this experiment to see the effect of drought on a stem.

You will need:

- flowers with single, straight stems
- scissors
- water
- two vases

1 You will need to buy some flowers with single, straight stems. Gerberas or tulips would be good flowers to use.

2 Ask an adult to carefully cut about 2 cm (about 1 in.) off the bottom of the flower stems. Divide your flowers into two groups.

3 Put one group of flowers into a vase and half-fill the vase with water. Put the other group of flowers into another vase. Do not put any water in this vase.

14

4 Over the next few days, watch what happens to the flowers. You may need to top up the water in the first vase.

5 What has happened to the flowers in the dry vase? Have they wilted? Their stems have not had water to keep their cells tight and strong, so they have bent over. The flowers in the wet vase should still be standing upright.

What next?

You could try a similar experiment using flowers with different kinds of stems – some thick, some thin, some smooth, some hairy. Place them all in dry vases. Which stems do you think will wilt first?

Growing stems

Stems grow from seeds. A tiny **shoot** pushes upwards out of the seed. It already has one or two little **seed leaves** that provide it with some food. The shoot becomes the stem, and starts growing new leaves. These make more food for the plant so that it can grow more.

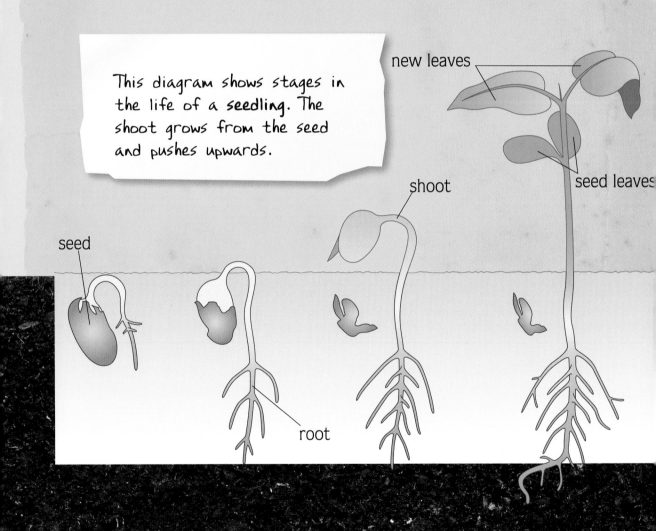

This diagram shows stages in the life of a seedling. The shoot grows from the seed and pushes upwards.

new leaves

shoot

seed leaves

seed

root

16

The buds along this cherry tree twig are opening up to become flowers.

Side shoots

As the stem grows upwards, little **buds** form along it. These then grow into side shoots, or leaves, or flowers. Some plants, such as tulips, don't have buds along their stems. Their leaves grow from the bottom of the stem and their flowers grow at the tip of the stem. On trees, side shoots, or twigs, eventually grow to become branches.

Speedy stems!

It can take many years for trees to grow tall. Some bamboo plants, though, have stems that grow very quickly. They have been recorded growing as much as 91 centimetres (about 36 inches) in one day!

Bendy stems, hard trunks

Many plant stems are covered with a thin layer of "skin". This is called the **epidermis**. It is strong but flexible.

Plants that live longer, such as shrubs and trees, have hardened stems. These are covered in a hard skin called **bark**.

These cotton grass stems are flexible enough to cope with being blown about by the wind.

Beautiful bark

Bark grows on shrubs and trees that live longer than a year or two. It protects the plant from diseases. It also stops the plant from drying out, and it helps to prevent animals nibbling the plant.

Bark is made of two layers. The inner layer grows and pushes the outer layer out. The outer layer is dead. It can look rough and cracked as the plant gets older. Different trees have different bark.

This person is stripping away the outer bark of a cork oak tree. The bark is made into corks for bottles, and corkboard. It will take around 10 years for the bark to grow back.

Fireproof coat

Some trees, such as giant sequoias, have bark that can protect the tree from fire. This means they can survive forest fires and lightning strikes, and can grow to enormous heights.

Many stems, no stems

Most plants have one single stem or trunk that grows up from the ground. Many also have side shoots or branches coming off the main stem.

This plant has many stems rising from the ground.

However, some plants have stems that branch off just above, or even below, the ground. These plants have many stems instead of one main stem.

No stems?

Some plants, such as aloe vera, look like they have no stems at all! Their leaves seem to grow straight from the ground. These plants do have stems, but they are very short and sometimes underground. Sometimes the stems can be very wide, such as on the welwitschia plant.

Coppicing

Sometimes people cut trees down, leaving just a stump on the ground. The tree then sends up lots of thinner stems from the stump. This is called coppicing. It is done to get more wood from one tree, and to control the height and shape of trees.

The welwitschia plant has a very short, thick stem. Its leaves look like they just rise out of the ground!

Underground stems

Some plants have stem parts that stay below the ground and have a special role. **Bulbs** are short, thick, underground stems. They are surrounded by soft scales that are the bottom ends of leaves.

You can see the swollen scales in this onion bulb.

These scales swell up with food. When the leaves die over winter, the bulb stays alive. The food in the bulb helps a new plant to grow in the spring.

Potatoes are grown and eaten all over the world.

Corms and tubers

Corms are similar to bulbs. They are swollen with food. However, this food is stored in the thick stem, not in the scales around it.

Tubers are swollen underground stem parts, attached to the stem by stalks. They store food to produce new plants. Potatoes are tubers. If you plant them, they will grow into new potato plants.

One bulb, many plants

Garlic bulbs are made up of separate sections called **cloves**. Each single clove can be broken off the bulb and planted to become a new garlic plant.

23

Sideways stems

Not all stems grow upwards! Some plants also grow stems that run sideways. Sideways stems growing above the ground are called **runners**, or **stolons**. Strawberry plants grow runners. They spread along the ground from the base of the stem. New young plants can start growing from buds on runners. They put down roots. Eventually, the runners connecting them to the main plant rot away.

You can see runners growing on these strawberry plants.

Rhizomes

Underground parts of the stem can grow sideways too. These sideways stems are called **rhizomes**. They are swollen with food so they can make new plants. When a new plant starts growing from a rhizome, the part connecting it to the old plant can rot away.

This diagram shows how rhizomes make new iris plants.

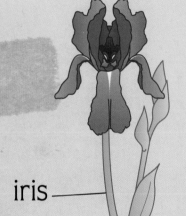

iris

new iris growing

rhizome

roots

Stem and trunk adaptations

Stems and trunks around the world can have special features. These are **adaptations** that help them to grow and survive.

Some plants grow thorns or spines along their stems. This helps to defend the plants against animals that might try to eat them.

The spines on this cactus plant help to stop animals from eating it.

In desert areas, cactus plants often have spines instead of leaves. These plants can make food in their stems. Some cactus stems have folds. This means they can swell up and store water in rainy times.

Upside-down trees

Baobab trees in Africa have very thick, bottle-shaped trunks. They store water here for the plant to use in dry seasons. They are sometimes called "upside-down trees". This is because their branches only have leaves for a very short time, and the rest of the time they look like roots.

Flowing by

Many plants growing in water have very soft, bendy stems. This means that they are not broken by water flowing past them. These stems would not be able to stand upright out of the water.

Stems, trunks, and us

We use stems and trunks in lots of ways. When a tree is cut down its trunk is called timber. We use timber for building lots of things, such as houses, fences, boats, and furniture. Telephone poles are made from single, straight trunks. We can use timber to make paper. Wood can also be burnt to give heat.

This sawmill has cut down trees to make planks of timber.

These machines are harvesting sugar cane plants to make sugar.

Stems to eat

We also eat some stems! Celery, rhubarb, onions, garlic, and potatoes are stem parts that we eat. We make spices from rhizomes of ginger and turmeric. We use the bark from cinnamon trees as a spice.

Sugar cane stems provide us with a very important substance – sugar. The stems are shredded and crushed, then soaked in water. The sugar in the stems dissolves in the water to make sugar juice. This is heated up so the water boils off and leaves demerara sugar crystals behind.

Musical stems

Bamboo stems are hard and hollow. They have been made into all kinds of musical instruments. People in China started making bamboo flutes in the Stone Age. Aborigines in Australia use them to make their long, straight didgeridoos.

Glossary

adaptation feature of a living thing that has changed over time to suit the environment

bark tough outer layer of trunks and branches that gives protection and strength

broadleaved tree with flat, wide leaves rather than thin needles. Trees with needles are called conifers.

bud swelling on a plant that can grow into new parts, such as leaves or a flower

bulb part of a plant's stem that stays underground, is surrounded by fleshy leaves, and can produce new plants

carbon dioxide gas with no colour or smell that is found in the air

cell tiny building block of life that all animals and plants are made of. Different kinds of cells do different jobs.

clove part of a bulb that can be broken off and can grow a new plant

conifer tree with cones and narrow leaves called needles. Pines and firs are conifers.

corm fleshy part of a plant's stem that stays underground and can produce new plants

drought long period of time with very little or no rain

epidermis outer layer of tough cells on a stem

heartwood centre part of a tree trunk that no longer transports water and sap

nutrient chemical that helps plants to live and grow

phloem tiny tubes in a plant that carry sap to all parts of the plant

rhizome stem part that grows sideways underground and can produce new plants

roots parts of plants that usually grow underground. They take water and nutrients from the soil, and hold the plant in the ground.

runner part of a plant that grows along the ground and sends roots into the ground, where it grows a new plant

sap liquid that contains food for all parts of a plant

sapwood newer, outer layers of wood in a trunk, between the bark and the heartwood, that transport water and sap

seed leaf one of usually two tiny leaves that form inside a seed and appear after a seed has germinated. Seed leaves are usually different shapes from the plant's leaves that grow later (true leaves).

seedling very young plant that has grown from a seed

shoot new growth on a plant, and also the first bit of a plant to grow from a germinated seed

stalk plant part that supports a leaf or a flower

stolon plant part that grows along the ground and can grow new plants

tendril special leaf or part of the stem that grows long and attaches to things to support the plant

tuber short, thick, roundish stem parts that grow underground and can produce new plants

xylem tiny tubes in a plant that carry water around the plant

Find out more

Books

Plants (Wildlife Watchers), Terry Jennings (QED, 2010)

Zoom! The Invisible World of Plants, Camilla de la Bedoyere (QED, 2012)

Websites

www.bbc.co.uk/nature/plants
This website has lots of information about plants. There are also some amazing film clips of plants all around the world.

www.rhs.org.uk/Children/For-kids/Mostest-plants Go to this web page to find out interesting facts about the tallest tree, smelliest flower, and speediest seed!

www.sciencekids.co.nz/plants.html
You can play games on this website, about how plants grow and the life cycle of plants.

Places to visit

The Royal Botanic Gardens in Kew in London has plants from all over the world.

The Eden Project in Cornwall is a series of huge domed greenhouses, one of which contains a rainforest! There are fun activities and amazing things to learn about plants.

Go for a walk in your local nature park! Spend time looking closely at all the different stems and trunks you can see.

Index